Way Of The Lightworker

Discovering Your Role &

Following Your Path

As A Healing Guide

By

Kelly Wallace

Professional Psychic Counselor

<u>DrKellyPsychic.com</u>[1]

© 2021 All Rights Reserved

Intuitive Living Publishing

Table of Contents

Books by Kelly Wallace

10 Minutes A Day to A Powerful New Life

Become Your Higher Self – Using Spiritual Energy to Transform Your Life

Breaking The Worry Habit – Stop Your Anxious Thoughts And Start Living!

Chakras – Heal, Clear, And Strengthen Your Energy Centers

Clear Your Karma – The Healing Power of Your Past Lives

Contacting Your Spirit Guides – Meeting and Working with Your Invisible Helpers

Creating A Charmed Life – Enchantments to Attract, Repel, Cleanse & Heal

Dream Work – Using The Wisdom Of Your Sleeping Mind To Change Your Waking Life

Energy Work – Heal, Cleanse, and Strengthen Your Aura

Everyday Miracles – Powerful Steps to Wonderful Experiences

Finding Your Life Purpose – Uncover Your Soul's True Goals

Healing the Child Within – Rewrite Your Early Childhood Life Script

How to Cure Candida – Yeast Infection Symptoms, Causes, Diet & Natural Remedies

Intuitive Living – Developing Your Psychic Gifts

Intuitive Tarot – Learn the Tarot Instantly

Is He The One? Finding And Keeping Your Soulmate

Master the Art of Picking Up Women

Master the Art of Dating Women

Master the Art of Sex and Seduction

Never Good Enough – Escaping The Prison Of Perfectionism

No-Sweat Homeschooling – The Cheap, Free, and Low-Stress Way to Teach Your Kids

Psychic Vampires – Protect and Heal Yourself from Energy Predators

Reprogram Your Subconscious – Use The Power Of Your Mind

Signs From The Universe – How To Recognize And Interpret These Life-Changing Messages

Spirit Guides And Healing Energy – Worth Your Guides, Aura, and Chakras

Spirits I Have Known – Haunted Places, Haunted People

Spiritual Alchemy – Transform Your Life and Everyone In It

The Art Of Happiness – Living A Life Of Peace And Simplicity

The Love You Deserve – Release Toxic Relationships and Attract Your Soulmate

The Mended Soul – Healing Your Mind, Body, & Spirit From Anxiety & Depression

The Overwhelmed Empath – A Guide For Sensitive Souls

The Power of Pets – How to Psychically Communicate with Your Pet

Transforming Your Money Mindset – From Broke To Abundance

True Wealth – Reprogram Your Subconscious for Financial Success

Upgrade Your Life – Small Changes, Easy Actions, Big Success

Way Of The Lightworker – Discovering Your Role & Following Your Path

Working With Your Angels – Contact Your Loving Guardians

About Kelly Wallace

Kelly is a bestselling spiritual and self-help author, former radio show host, and has been a professional psychic counselor for over twenty years. She can see, hear, sense, and feel information sent from Spirit, the Universe, and a client's Higher Self.

Whether your problems or concerns center on love, finances, family, career, health, education, or your purpose in life, she writes books that will help you easily make lasting changes.

Kelly also offers professional psychic counseling, caring guidance, and solutions that work! More than just a typical psychic reading or counseling session, you will feel you've found a real friend during your time of need—whether you simply want answers and guidance to your current worries or concerns, or you're interested in learning more about your soulmate, spirit guides, angels, past lives, or anything else.

Contact her today for an in-depth and life-altering reading!

Website: DrKellyPsychic.com[1]

Email: Dr.Kelly.Psychic.Counselor@gmail.com

---

1. http://psychicreadingsbydrkelly.webs.com/

What This Book Covers

The Way Of The Lightworker

People all over the world are becoming more enlightened as outworn beliefs are being discarded, replaced with new discoveries and open minds. This shift in awareness is naturally calling forth more and more Lightworkers.

As we increase in numbers, so, too, will the power of our collective consciousness. It will raise positive vibrations across the world and lift everything and everyone up. We, Lightworkers, will lead others into a higher level of knowing and living. Can you imagine what that means for all of us as humans, as souls, and for our planet? Wow!

What Is A Lightworker?

The easiest way to describe a Lightworker is someone who feels a strong need to help people, animals, or nature. These spiritual souls are very much like angels on Earth, doing whatever they can, big or small, to serve in some way.

A Lightworker is sensitive down to their very core and often feels deeply sad when they encounter any being that's in distress. Even as children they've been kinder and more compassionate than most of their peers. They want to do all they can to make things good and right in the world and often choose paths where their empathy can be put to good use.

You'll often see Lightworkers in careers as nurses, veterinarians, teachers, speakers, writers, artists, or anywhere else where they can assist others in need and help them to heal or to see their own light within.

They don't have to think about why they're drawn to healing and helping paths, it's a drive that never fades and only becomes stronger as the years go by. Their natural gift of intuition allows them to understand how others feel with great empathy and they perceive the world around them as a place that needs to be healed on so many levels. Their goal, whether consciously or unconsciously, is to erase as much negativity as possible. That's a tall order to fill and some Lightworkers can become overwhelmed and disillusioned, though most keep moving forward.

Anyone Can Be A Lightworker

Not all Lightworkers are aware of their life purpose from the start though some are born knowing that a helping and healing path is at the center of their very being. Others don't discover this until later in life, usually as a result of tragedy, illness, trauma, or struggle that brings about an awakening.

Eventually, they all sense a driving need to use their compassion and insight to support others in some way. Plain and simple, their mission is to make a positive impact on the Earth in any way they can.

Nearly all Lightworkers have faced more than their share of heartache, abuse, illness, and injury. They're very aware that they have a shadow side, even if they haven't worked on making peace with this part of themselves. This wounded, darker side is often what leads them to their true calling in life, even if they aren't exactly sure how or where to help.

Whether their role in life is modest or huge, every Lightworker is a bridge between this world and the hereafter. And whether they lead a throng of people or one at a time, the goal is to bring others to a higher state of living and loving.

For too long most humans have been living their lives unconsciously, but with everything that's been happening (Covid pandemic, climate change, poverty, hunger, war, etc.) it's clear that change is needed. I believe that a global awakening has already started. You bought this book because you either know for certain or sense that you're one of the souls who can heal and help and lead the way to a better future. It won't happen overnight, but slow and steady wins the race.

So what kind of Lightworker are you? Are you a newly awakened Lightworker who wants to be of service somehow? Or are you a long-time Lightworker who came into this life knowing who you are and what you need to do? Are you ready and eager to jump into your role? Have you been a helper and healer for some time? Or have you hidden this very important part of yourself from the world out of fear or uncertainty?

Wherever you're at on your journey, I'm so glad that you've made the decision to explore and embrace your true calling in life. The world needs you!

Lightworkers Are Born and Made

There are two ways people become Lightworkers: they either come into this life knowing from the start what they're meant to do, or something significant happens that wakes them up and leads them down this path. When a Lightworker acknowledges their life purpose it's usually impossible to ignore it. Their consciousness is forever shifted and there's an instinctual need to answer this calling. Some healing guides might easily accept their role and quickly make dramatic life changes while others move along slowly until they feel more confident.

For those who are born Lightworkers they've been doing their work for several lifetimes, even if they don't remember them. If most of their past lives, or the most recent one, were filled with persecution though they might find it difficult to embrace their role as a Lightworker. Even so, they can't deny the pulling sensation in their soul telling them they have important work to do.

There are so many people on this Earth right now who have incarnated yet again to help others and even more who are just now waking up to their mission in life. It can be a long and difficult process though, especially if they've built up walls to protect and hide themselves. Revealing who they truly are and what they want to do in life can be a scary process. They worry about being made fun of, wonder if they truly are special and meant to help heal the world, and question if it's all worth it. Of course, they can't deny their true purpose and it really is worth it—and then some.

One of the things I've heard again and again from Lightworkers is what type of education they need, what tests they should pass, or what proof they need to "know for sure" if this is their true calling in life. Yes, to be a nurse, a veterinarian, and some other career choices takes years of formal education. For the vast majority of us though all you need is a devotion to bringing goodness into the world. As long as you're living as your authentic self, operating through your light, and helping others in some way, *you are a Lightworker.*

Common Lightworker Traits

Just the fact that you're curious about this subject shows that you're a Lightworker. Someone who has no desire to help other beings wouldn't be interested in this information. Even so, you still might want to know if you truly are meant to be a Lightworker. What are some of the "symptoms" we experience?

Let me share a list of common traits most of us have in common. Not everyone will identify with everything on this list, but I bet after reading it you'll see just how deep that calling in your soul truly is.

1. You've always questioned rules and traditions.

2. Injustice and inequality deeply hurt and anger you.

3. Your goals and dreams have always been big.

4. You know that there's always an easier and more peaceful way to do things.

5. In your soul you know that we're not alone in this Universe.

6. You've experienced more pain, trauma, tragedy, and darkness than many others have.

7. You have a natural desire to learn about positive and progressive topics.

8. You've always had a strong need for harmony and bringing people together.

9. Having a positive influence on others fills you with happiness and satisfaction.

10. You have a deep desire to help causes that are important to you.

11. You're naturally intuitive and can sense energy shifts and emotions in others.

12. You feel connected with all living beings and the Earth.

13. You feel as if you're on the outside looking in and have always been somewhat of a loner.

14. You know you're here for a higher purpose.

15. People come to you for advice and often tell you things they wouldn't tell others.

16. You've always been wise beyond your years and people have probably said so.

17. You're naturally spiritual and philosophical. You see things far more deeply than others do.

18. You're sensitive to other people's energy, and can only take it in small doses.

19. You're always looking for ways to improve your life and the lives of others.

20. You see what needs to be fixed or changed and do what you can to make it happen.

21. Rather than forcing your beliefs on others, you focus on showing them their own power.

22. You're naturally creative and your talents might involve cooking, art, writing, or music.

23. People have told you that you're an old soul. You know you've lived many lifetimes.

24. You don't fully fit in with your family and friends. The proverbial black sheep.

25. You have a knack for manifesting things in your life. (Depending on what you focus on this can be good or bad. Lightworkers are very sensitive and too often manifest hardships.)

26. You're naturally drawn to ancient spiritual information and history.

27. You feel a strong connection with nature.

28. You've experienced one or more spiritual awakenings that have changed you in some way.

29. You know you've lived many lives and hope this is your last. (Yes, Lightworkers get tired and discouraged!)

I'm sure after reading over that list you can pinpoint several things proving that you're a Lightworker. Realizing your true purpose can be both exciting and stressful. Try not to worry too much about the details and just be confident in the fact that once you embrace your role as a guide and healer, your path will unfold naturally.

Shining Your Light

As a Lightworker, you can choose how and where to shine your light. There are healing guides who are parents, teachers, painters, exercise instructors, counselors, social workers, forest rangers, life coaches, bloggers, and many other professions. Lightworkers can be in any role, in any field, in any part of the world. You can easily spot them because they all help in some way.

Regardless of what path you want to take, the world needs your light! You came into this life to complete your mission. In fact, you've probably been doing this for centuries.

Whenever uncertainty washes over you, remind yourself that you have everything you need to do the work you're meant to do. If you don't, such as the case with a profession that requires higher learning, you can always pursue this education if it's something you feel compelled to do.

Where Do You Start?

Your first step as a Lightworker is to focus on healing yourself. While it's true that most of us are "wounded healers" you still need to help yourself before you can help others. I've seen far too many counselors, social workers, even doctors, and religious leaders, project their own mental and emotional wounds onto others. Not only is this unfair and unhelpful to the people who need you, but it also stunts your own growth.

We want to be as healed and whole as possible before embarking on this path. That doesn't mean you need years of therapy or have to be completely at peace with everything in your past. As long as you continually work on yourself you'll be able to serve others far better. You can work on this by yourself through books, diet, exercise, and whatever else appeals to you, or through the assistance of a professional.

I've written a few books on self-healing: *Shadow Work – Understanding and Making Peace With Your Darker Side*, and *Healing The Child Within – Changing Your Early Childhood Life Script*. If you haven't read them yet, they're a good place to start. There are also many other wonderful books available, as well as professional therapists, spiritual counselors, life coaches, and more. I believe that we all gravitate toward a personal healing path that feels right for us.

Knowing When You're Ready

You know in your soul that you're meant to be a Lightworker. Somehow, someway, you want to help guide or heal others. But how do you know you're ready? Some people just jump in right away, while others are a bit nervous and uncertain as to when the time is right. Here are a few clues that are proof positive you're ready to start your journey.

1. You Feel That Time Is Running Out

Although the soul is infinite, and regardless of your current age, you could have had this nagging feeling for a while that the clock is ticking. You need and want to do something *now*. You feel you've wasted your time on things that don't matter nearly as much as helping others in some way.

You might have felt this way since you were a child, young adult, or perhaps only recently, and at times it can make you feel depressed, anxious, eager, or conflicted. You might know exactly what you want to do, haven't figured it out yet, or are afraid to get started. Even so, there's a pulling sensation inside that you must follow.

This feeling of time running out and all this wasted time is not only uncomfortable, but it can become so heavy that nothing satisfies you like it used to. Not until you act on your life's mission will these feelings subside. Until they do, it's a constant reminder that you're here to do more.

2. You Feel The Calling

Even if you don't know what it is just yet, you know you have a greater life purpose. This calling gets stronger and louder as the months and years go by. You might have read books and articles, perhaps even gotten psychic readings, trying to figure out exactly what your life purpose is. You've been curious about it and have spent a lot of time thinking about why you're here and what you're meant to do.

The Universe wants you to wake up and become conscious of your life journey as a Lightworker, to embrace it and start acting on it. Once you do, you'll find that you can accomplish so much more than you have in the past. The only limitations are the ones we set for ourselves. It's so easy to get in your own way, to trip yourself up, or abandon your purpose altogether. But when you realize what your true calling is and begin pursuing it, you can transform your entire life.

This is exactly what happened to me. It's almost like I've been two different people. I was a mother and housewife, working menial jobs, unhappy in my marriage, feeling very lost, yet knowing I was meant for something bigger and better.

Not until I was in my 30s, after far too many hardships and heartbreaks, did I take my blinders off and admit that I had a deep need to help others. The path was long, with many twists and turns, and a whole lot of learning and exploring until I became the person I am today. And, I'm still growing and finding ways to reach others in bigger or different ways.

3. You Feel Like An Alien Or Outsider

Every Lightworker I've met has told me they've always felt they don't belong on this planet. It's like being an alien plopped down into a foreign world. You might feel distant from people, like you don't really fit in, or as if you're watching others through a window. That doesn't mean you don't love or feel loved. It doesn't mean you don't have friends or other close relationships.

The main thing is, we just feel different and always have. It could be the way we think, the way we view things, or our philosophy on certain subjects. A lot of times, what's normal social interaction and custom for everyone else feels strange or forced when we do it.

Many of us feel that our families don't really accept or understand us, and we may only have had a few close friends. We feel overlooked, misunderstood, or completely invisible. Too many of us are labeled as weird, anti-social, and are wrongly judged. That will all change though once you start following your calling as a Lightworker.

As healing guides, we want nothing more than to change archaic beliefs, tear down old social structures, and live in a world filled with peace, freedom, unconditional love, and acceptance. We know that might never happen on a global scale, but we do what we can where we can.

4. You Want To Save The World

You're saddened, tired, and angry with the way the world works. It pains us to see people or animals suffering, and cuts deeply knowing how nature is being crowded out and wiped out, while the Earth itself is struggling under the heavy burden of its human inhabitants.

We know we've come here to save the world in some way. It's a huge task though and one that's so overwhelming that some Lightworkers choose to rush back to the life they've known for far too long and ignore their true mission.

Whenever I feel overwhelmed by the fact that I'm here to help heal and guide as many people as possible and do what I can for the planet, I take a deep breath and remind myself that I'm not the only Lightworker. There are millions of us! I'm not doing this alone and you won't either. When you doubt yourself just remember that it's your fearful ego talking and not your ancient and ever-wise soul.

5. Your Shadow Side Is Surfacing

Our main goal is to transform darkness into light. The closer you are to following your path as a Lightworker the more your own darkness will start making itself known. Rather than squashing it down, know that this is a wonderful sign showing that you're that much closer to your true calling. In fact, even as you pursue your life purpose, those dark parts will bubble up from time to time. Consider this a challenge, a sign that some part of you is ready to heal and change. In turn, this will help you to do even better work.

It's easy to shove aside people and events that have wounded us. We get so good at it, in fact, that we sometimes can't remember what tragic event happened or we deny it altogether. But when the time is right it will stare you in the face. This Shadow Work should be viewed as a blessing and opportunity to heal and grow.

Why is it that Lightworkers usually have the darkest lives? It seems unfair, doesn't it? We haven't had the luxury of easy lives because we've been in training since our first breath, whether in this life or many others, to recognize suffering in various forms. Simply put, if we've never seen something we won't know what it looks like. Without experiencing so much darkness how would we ever know how to transmute it into light?

For a lot of us, this Shadow Work comes in the form of resolving family karma. In my own case, I've liberated myself and my children from many generations of unhealthy patterns and broke the chain of abuse and addiction.

Facing that darkness can often feel like a huge burden and something best swept under the rug—yet again. But the best thing to do is work on healing yourself first then the rest will fall into place. Once you feel stronger, happier, and healthier it will be easier to help family members or, if it's for your highest good, to cut ties completely.

6. You Notice How Good You Are At Manifesting

When we think of manifesting the first things that come to mind are wealth, health, love, success, and happiness. When you look back on your life though you might find that very little, or none, of that is true. I can guarantee that you're a powerful manifestor though. How? Because, with your high level of energy you have materialized everything you've been afraid of or have become used to.

Take a look at everything you have right now—the good, the bad, and the ugly. The more "negative" things you have in your life actually show just how powerful you truly are, you just need to learn how to direct your energy differently.

The moment you were an adult and out of your parents' home is the moment you became responsible for your life and how you use your energy. Unconsciously, you created what you have now so that it was in alignment with all you've known, feared, or expected from life and others. Once you admit to yourself that you're truly a Lightworker and deserve better you can then begin to change your life in many ways.

7. You're Empathy Is Getting Stronger

This might seem contrary but every Lightworker is an empath yet not every empath is a Lightworker. All empaths feel the suffering of others, of animals, of nature. They can also feel immense happiness and love. It's easy to mistake the feelings of others for your own emotions but in reality, you've just picked up on some other energy.

Yet not all people with strong emotions like this are meant to travel the road as a healer or guide. They just go through life feeling deeply and very often not knowing why or what to do with it. I believe that in the future they'll come back as Lightworkers though. Perhaps they're in training or are working on some past life or present life karmic issues at the moment. Also, they don't feel an immense need to help others as Lightworkers do.

With Lightworkers, it's essential to be an empath because you can't heal or fix what you can't feel in yourself. It's like people who have never been married trying to be a marriage counselor. Sure, they can read all the books, go to the best university, and get a fancy degree, but if they haven't experienced it they won't be as effective as those who have.

There have been times when I've cursed the fact that I feel so deeply, yet more often than not I consider it a blessing. I love the fact that I can not only feel my own emotions so strongly but also those of my family, my pets, even the plants in my garden. For us, it's like we live on a whole other plane of existence.

8. You Become More Interested In Ancient History or Teachings

You've probably always been drawn to certain parts of history, ancient thoughts or beliefs, or healing practices. As you get closer to your true life's work you'll find that these interests escalate. You can't get enough. You could suddenly find yourself learning all you can about Ancient Egypt or Ancient Greece, crystal healing, herbal medicine, the tarot, astrology, or any other age-old practice.

As a Lightworker you'll naturally gravitate toward esoteric subjects, searching for answers and direction. You derive strength and confidence from other Lightworkers in the past, even if you don't continue to follow this course.

When I first started out on my life's mission I learned everything from reflexology to art therapy, healing with essential oils and herbs, to hypnotherapy and NLP. I couldn't learn fast enough as I searched, almost obsessively, for that one moment when it would all click into place and show me the way. In the end, becoming a psychic counselor fit me perfectly and I've used much of what I've learned over the years in my practice.

9. You Feel More Connected To A Higher Power

Regardless of what higher power you believe in now or always have believed in, the more you embrace your light the stronger this connection becomes. You know there's something greater than just this human race, just this one life, and have even seen God/Spirit/Light working in your life and felt it moving through you at times.

10. People With Problems Gravitate Toward You

Lightworkers always seem to attract people with problems and/ or challenging personalities. They could be friends, family members, coworkers, or complete strangers who sense your light and feel the need to dump on you in some way. That's not always a bad thing, since, as helpers, we instinctively want to heal others, but it can be draining at times as well.

People will naturally want to unload their complaints, vent about how unfair life has been to them, talk about their dysfunctional relationships, health problems, money problems, and the list goes on. You want to be sympathetic and offer advice—though it's rarely followed—but too often, people like this are energy vampires who take and take without giving much, if anything, in return.

Of course, you're kindhearted to a fault, and if you can help someone you will. However, you need to know when and where to set boundaries for your own well-being. Sometimes you might have to cut ties if someone is far too negative and you're constantly feeling drained or anxious after having been around them. At the very least, you should spend as little time with them as possible.

11. Your Emotional Ups And Downs Intensify

When you're feeling good you have more energy, life is flowing effortlessly, and you feel wide open in heart, mind, and soul. In these moments you have a strong connection to Spirit and you can see your purpose clearly. You pursue goals with ease and everything seems to be happily falling into place. Then suddenly your mood shifts and you feel depressed or anxious. (Depression and/or anxiety is extremely common in Lightworkers.)

When you feel down you subconsciously cut yourself off from your higher purpose. Life comes to a standstill or things start falling apart. Negative thoughts play over and over in your mind and you might even fall back into unhealthy habits or patterns. These dark times might last days, weeks, or months.

Those highs and lows can be discouraging, but when you're going through a rough patch remind yourself that it's a sign that you need to get back on your path as a Lightworker. Even if you have to "fake it until you make it". Giving in to the darkness only makes it worse.

From personal experience, I know how deep we can get into the abyss or our emotions, and sometimes it feels nearly impossible to pull ourselves out. Rest assured, that like the Wheel of Fortune tarot card, you'll be on an upswing again soon. And, the more you follow your true calling in life, you'll find that the bad times don't stick around as long and you get through them much easier.

12. You've Been Having Odd Dreams

The dream world is almost always a strange place, but when your soul is opening up more you'll find that your dreams start changing.

- You could have dreams about events in your past as your subconscious works on healing these old wounds and letting go.

- You might start having lucid dreams where you can control your surroundings, events, and people.

- You could dream of traveling to the homes of friends or relatives, other countries, or even visit the Astral Plane.

- You might have dreams of past lives or even future lives.

- Loved ones and pets that have crossed over might start showing up in your dreams as well.

If you've experienced some, several, or all of these, it's a sure sign that your path as a Lightworker is on the near horizon, if you haven't started following it already. I know that some of these "symptoms" might be uncomfortable or even downright depressing or painful, though I try to remind myself that we all need to go through growing pains in life. If every path was easy we would never learn the lessons we need to for our Lightworker paths.

Different Types Of Lightworkers

Every Lightworker has their own unique strengths and talents. Nobody else on this planet—past, present, or future—has walked in your shoes. The lessons you've learned and experiences you've had make you different from other Lightworkers, just as they're different from you.

The world can never have too many healing guides because we all offer a personal viewpoint. And, the events that have shaped your life will direct you to the type of Lightwork that will come naturally to you.

These are the main types of Lightworker categories, the ones most people are drawn to. So what kind of Lightworker are you? You'll likely possess at least one of the following traits and could even have one or more other talents as well.

1. Healers

If you feel compelled to help others mentally, physically, emotionally, or spiritually then you fall into this category. Whether you want to use hands-on healing, herbal remedies, physical therapy, counseling, nursing, writing, childcare, speaking, or other modalities you know that your goal is to heal. You naturally and quickly ease the pain or suffering of animals or people.

One drawback to being a healer is unless you learn to ground and protect yourself you can feel overwhelmed, tired, anxious, or depressed after a session. It's not uncommon for a healer to take on the affliction of their client whether for hours, days, or longer. It takes a conscious effort to create boundaries and keep yourself strong and healthy on all levels.

2. Psychics

Some Lightworkers are born with psychic abilities such as clairvoyance, clairaudience, divination, or mediumship. It's an innate talent that you expand on throughout life and use to help others, whether you do so professionally or not. Others develop one or more of these gifts after going through a life-altering event. I've known people who realized their newfound abilities only after an accident, illness, or trauma. It's like the event woke up a part of their psyche that had been asleep all those years.

Many psychics can predict future events, relay a client's past lives, or offer guidance on the most beneficial path for the person. Any psychic who's a true Lightworker will always use their talents to help people reach the most positive outcome, realize their goals, and promote peace and goodwill.

3. Messengers

Some Lightworkers have a strong need to spread important information to others. Their goal is to relay truth, love, and peace while helping to enlighten others. Their inner light shines and, like a magnet, people are naturally attracted to them and their work. They're persuasive, kind, and charismatic, using their abilities for positive change.

They can make a great impact on the world through communicating their messages whether as public speakers, teachers, writers, musicians, life coaches, and so on. The goal of these messengers is to serve others through their words, actions, or work.

4. Manifestors

These people are excellent at channeling their visions and energy to attract what they want in life and for others. They want nothing more than to make the world a better place for people, animals, or nature. You might see them as business owners, and, like other Lightworker categories, they can also be teachers, instructors, speakers, etc.

5. Transmuters

Also known as Neutralizers, their goal is to dispel negativity. They take bad situations, whether due to human mistakes, accidents, or disasters, and do something good with them. They're able to face trauma, darkness, and challenges without flinching and can find ways to turn it into something positive or productive even if the situation seems hopeless at first. Ultimately, they want to restore balance or leave a person or situation better off than before.

These types are naturally drawn to work in places of high conflict, crisis management, or emergency services. I've also seen them in roles as dietitians, exercise instructors, even paranormal investigators.

You don't need to choose one of the above categories to pursue your Lightwork since many of us end up doing one, some, or all of these things and don't really need to label it. It comes naturally and we go where we feel compelled to. In myself I can see how I typically follow at least three of those Lightworker paths at the same time.

To sum it up, Lightworkers are awakened people who have a strong need to help all living beings and the Earth itself. At their cores they're kind and dedicated, using their higher mental, physical, emotional, and/or spiritual energy levels to support and serve others.

As we talked about earlier, not all Lightworkers realize their purpose or potential from the beginning. When they do though it can sometimes create a dramatic shift in their life and sweeping changes. For others, they may continue to lead their current life, stay in their current career, yet find ways to help by creating positive experiences whenever and wherever they can. No heartfelt deed is too small.

We Attract Dysfunctional Relationships

One of the most difficult areas for Lightworkers in their own lives is intimate relationships. It's so natural for us to give, and give, and give so much more while forgetting that we also deserve to receive love, support, and nurturing in return. Loving and being loved is a natural cycle of energy and one where we often struggle.

Since we *are* healers we attract those who need healing, and this is especially true when it comes to romantic partnerships. We don't think about fixing someone, healing them, or helping them to be the best version of themselves, it's a subconscious need to do so. The problem here is that we always put our partner's needs before our own and this creates an imbalance.

To make matters worse, Lightworkers are empaths, so they easily become overwhelmed by the emotions and toxicity of others. As you can imagine, or have experienced, this keeps us in dysfunctional patterns for years, if not decades. Hopefully, in time, we finally recognize that, although we want to help, it isn't a healthy situation and it isn't what true love should be like.

If a Lightworker is unable to heal themselves, create boundaries, and ultimately find a healthy relationship, they'll either stay in their toxic union or completely close themselves off as a way to protect their sensitive spirit. Once you shut down it can be difficult, if not impossible, to recognize positive love let alone opening yourself up to receiving it.

For some, it can also close off their spiritual healing gifts, while doing further harm to their already shaky self-esteem and self-worth. In a vicious cycle, it makes them even more vulnerable to toxic relationships or a lifetime of loneliness. It's not like this for all Lightworkers, but for many of us, it is.

Realizing that, because you're naturally a helper and healer, you're going to attract "broken" people is the first step to healing yourself. After being closed off for so long though it might feel strange when you're finally in a healthy relationship. Everything about the partnership will set off alarm bells in your mind because you simply aren't used to it. Before embarking on a new relationship and especially once you're in a positive union, some things that are helpful to keep in mind are:

- Identifying where you've been blocked

- Identifying your strengths

- Being honest with what you need to be fulfilled

- Learning how to ask for what you need

- Allowing yourself to receive healthy love

- Being gentle with yourself when your fears rise to the surface

- Keeping the lines of communication open between you and your partner

- Respecting and caring for yourself first and foremost

- Creating healthy boundaries

When you start living your life as the Lightworker you truly are and fulfilling your life purpose it will be easier to find healthy love. Typically, when we deny this part of ourselves or aren't living this path to the fullest is when we're in our most dysfunctional relationships.

When You Grow And Your Partner Doesn't

You and your significant other have been together for some time now and started off strong but somewhere along the way you've drifted apart. Maybe the love is still there or perhaps it's turned into indifference, anger, or sadness. This is a common theme with many Lightworkers as they begin exploring their purpose more.

The reason it happens is because you used to operate at the level of your lower Earth-self and that's the person who made this relationship choice. As time went on though your higher Spiritual-self grew and the Lightworker you're meant to be started stretching and growing more each day.

Now that you've been awakened your current relationship might not meet your needs since your partner is on one plane and you're now on a completely different one. You could still have a deep love for your partner but you might not be *in* love with them anymore. This can bring up feelings of guilt and confusion.

Soon you'll need to make a decision. Do you want to stay in the relationship and work on things? Or would you be better off going your separate ways? Neither path is easy and you'll need to choose what works best for you. I've known clients who have stayed together and made it work, others that stayed together but chose to live in separate homes, others who have parted ways with the love and friendship intact, and still others who waited until things deteriorated so badly that they had an "excuse" to break things off.

To be honest, I've done each one of those. In the end, parting ways with the love still intact and remaining friends has been my best decision. It was just too difficult to stay with someone whose outlook on life and spirituality was the complete opposite of mine and who wasn't growing at all while I was changing in so many ways. It doesn't make him a bad person and we had many wonderful years together.

When our paths divided too drastically though I knew it was time to let the relationship go. It was sad and difficult, I grieved then eventually healed over time. I've never regretted the breakup though. More than 15 years since our first meeting we're still close friends. He's living his life on his terms and I'm living mine on my terms.

Before making any decision though, be sure that you understand your own unique purpose in this world and the reason why you attracted this relationship in the first place. Everyone is brought into our lives for a purpose. They're learning something from us and we're learning something from them.

Using myself as an example and the relationship I just mentioned, he gave me the confidence and freedom to explore my path as a Lightworker. Without him, I don't know if I would have had the courage to pursue my psychic business and writing full time. In turn, I helped him to be more open and loving in a relationship and also with his children. He's always told me how much I've helped him to be a better man.

Finding Love That Matches Your Soul

Along your journey, you'll find that as your energy frequency increases you'll attract and be attracted to like-minded people. When you start finding these people it means that you're releasing past life and present life karma. You're healing and growing at a soul level. Because of this, you'll draw in these types of people:

- Those who are in your core soul group

- Those who are in an outer group but still kindred spirits

- Those who are attracted to your energy field but aren't in either group

When looking for love it's best to choose souls from the first two groups since your energy frequencies vibrate higher. You'll mesh well, even if you challenge one another at times. It goes without saying that you should avoid people from the last soul group only because they aren't Lightworkers and their vibration is much lower than yours.

Also, something you'll want to be awake to is that people in the last category will naturally be attracted to your light. Since you're a healer guide, you might feel compelled to help them, even if this is on a purely subconscious level. This isn't necessarily a bad thing, except in the case of intimate relationships.

It's incredibly rare for this type of partnership to work out only because you're both coming from two vastly different planes. Living day and night with someone on a lower soul level and trying to help lift them up is exhausting and very often fruitless. I learned that lesson the hard way in my second marriage. It was the worst seven years of my adult life.

We need all kinds of people in our lives but we also need to decide who we share our energy with, especially when it comes to intimacy. Just as people are positively influenced by our energy, we're also influenced by theirs—for the good and bad. When you're with someone who operates at a lower frequency they can pull you down with them. Some clues that a person is on a lower soul level are:

- Anger issues

- Any type of addiction

- Financial problems

- Always between jobs

- Main focus is on sex and/or money

- Unwilling or unable to participate in open communication

- Placing blame on everyone else

- Constant complaining

- Always down on their luck

- Irresponsible in one or more areas of their life

- Problems with commitment

- Exhibits immaturity in one or more ways

- Values physical objects over everything else

- Very secretive

- Chronic liar

- Poor hygiene

- Unconcerned with their health

As you can imagine, the list could go on but those are some of the major red flags you should be aware of when seeking out a relationship. Lightworkers are sensitive and accepting to a fault and we too often ignore these glaring signs that someone isn't right for us. Once you're fully awakened and following your true path you wouldn't even think of choosing someone with any of the above traits as a significant other.

Don't beat yourself up though if you have been, are, or soon get into a relationship with someone like this. It takes time and awareness to know your worth and spot someone who's on a lower vibrational level. Many times, people are chameleons and put on a good act for a while, though eventually, their true colors will show. Whether we want to admit it to ourselves or not, we've always sensed that something just wasn't right.

The problem is, we live in a society that shuns or just doesn't understand intuition. If things look good on the surface then it should be good enough. And, if so many other things about this person seem so right it's easy to become infatuated and ignore the voice within telling us otherwise.

Never doubt your gut feelings that tell you something or someone isn't for your highest good, even if you don't have proof and even if they seem like "such a nice or misunderstood person". You don't owe anything to anyone except yourself. Staying in a relationship that isn't healthy or that you aren't happy in only wastes time and drags you down.

As a Lightworker, you're meant to be with someone on your same wavelength. Or, if you choose to be single for a while or even a lifetime, if it's for the right reasons, then that's perfectly fine too. It's when we do things and put up with things for the wrong reasons that cause the most problems in life.

We need to change our way of thinking from *what* love is to what the *purpose* of love is. When we view it this way, it's much easier to attract a positive partner. Ask yourself what the purpose of love is and with some thought, I'm sure you can come up with things that might surprise you or wake you up.

For many people, the thought of love could mean not being alone, having similar interests, flowers, nice gifts, a beautiful home, kids, marriage, awe-inspiring vacations, amazing sex, someone who will cook and clean and rub your feet, etc.

While none of those are actually negative, when we view love at a soul level it's vastly different. It means you feel calm when around them, you respect each other, you balance each other out, you support each other to grow and learn and be your best. You can be yourself, you feel secure in the relationship, you aren't afraid of having tough conversations, and you help each other.

Love that's at a higher soul level is never solely based on sex, romance, good looks, or material things, though it can certainly be part of the package. The journey of a Lightworker is often complex and being with someone who isn't a positive match for you makes things even more difficult. Instead, having a partner who's on your same energy level will help to amplify your vibrational state which will help you help others better.

Self-Care Is A Must

As a Lightworker, your light shines brightest when you're connected to and tuned in to a higher frequency. The following self-care tips are the very ones I use in my own life to help keep me balanced and at my best. Nothing on the list is anything you absolutely must do so feel free to pick and choose whatever resonates with you right now. Over time, you can adopt more of these ideas, adjust them, find your own, and let go of any that don't fit into your lifestyle.

1. Connect With A Higher Source

Every morning before I get out of bed and each night before I go to sleep I take just a few minutes to meditate. Sometimes I'll do a guided meditation that I have on a phone app, and other times I'll just let my mind go where it wants to. Or, I'll focus on things I'm grateful for, positive things that have happened recently, goals I have, or I just clear my mind and breathe.

Many books, articles, and spiritual teachers recommend 15 minutes or more, but I've found that even 5 minutes a day can do wonders for my mood and well-being. And you don't need to do anything formal because meditation, in any way you choose to do it, raises your vibration. As a result, this helps to put you into the right frequency to attract positive people, opportunities, and experiences. It releases all that pent-up energy and gets it flowing smoothly again. Think of it like recharging your Lightworker batteries.

2. Ground Yourself

When you're feeling overwhelmed or stressed, or your thoughts are jumbled or racing, grounding yourself can help calm and center you again. There are many ways to ground but some of my favorite activities are:

- Taking a walk in nature

- Sitting on a big rock at a park and absorbing the sights and sounds around me

- Walking barefoot in the grass or sand

- Brushing or petting my dog

- Running my hands over the trunk of a tree then sitting with my back against it

- Taking in slow, deep breaths and letting them out twice as slowly for a few minutes

- Taking a shower, a bath, or swimming in a pool

- Getting out my crayons and pad of paper then drawing whatever comes to mind, or just doodling

- Getting out my markers and mandala coloring book and getting lost in that for a while

- Lying on my bed or sitting in my chair with my eyes closed listening to soothing music or nature sounds

- Looking out my bedroom window and watching the birds and squirrels and just absorbing the view

- Making a pot of homemade soup, smelling it while it simmers, then enjoying a big bowlful

- Doing a short yoga routine for 5 or 10 minutes

These ideas are just a jumping-off place for you. Over time I'm sure you'll discover your own personal ways of grounding yourself and recharging.

3. Clearing Your Energy Field

Whether you intentionally interact with others as a Lightworker or regularly come into contact with people through work and daily activities, their vibrations can creep into your own energy field and pollute it. It's not intentional, but it's easy for Lightworkers to attract and hold onto those lower frequencies.

If you don't focus on clearing yourself, all of that energy that isn't yours will accumulate and eventually affect you. You could find yourself feeling fatigued, have problems with insomnia, nightmares, headaches, irritability, depression, and a long list of other "phantom ailments". (I call them phantom ailments only because the symptoms didn't originate in your own mind or body but came from someone else.)

When you work on cleansing your energy field you'll see how much better you feel. Imagine your house being tightly shut all winter then spring comes and you're able to open all the windows and let in the sunshine and fresh air. That sounds great, doesn't it? But how do you go about doing this?

Meditation and Visualization

You can do a simple daily meditation where you sit somewhere quiet, close your eyes, and take a few deep, slow breaths. When you feel relaxed, visualize a cleansing white light entering through the top of your head, filling your entire body all the way to your toes. Then imagine this white light spreading several inches or even several feet outside of your body. Take your time and stay with this as long as you want to.

This light begins to swirl around like a whirlpool, collecting all of the debris in your energy field that's been left there by others. The light spins faster and slowly starts to exit through the soles of your feet.

Keep visualizing the light moving down, down, down, until it's completely left your body. You can then imagine this "dirty light" going off into the universe to be cleansed or into the center of the Earth to be disintegrated.

When you finish, your energy field is cleansed and you should feel a sense of silence and expansion. I'm almost always surprised at how all of that chatter I felt in my mind and aura is calmed after doing this brief exercise. As Lightworkers, it's often hard to know what's our stuff and what we've taken on that belongs to others.

Physical Movement

Moving your body in a calm, controlled, and flowing way will help to rebalance, recharge, and cleanse your energy field. Some of the best exercises for this are walking outdoors, stretching, yoga, tai chi, qigong, and just moving your body to gentle music.

4. Shine Light On Your Shadows

I haven't met a Lightworker yet who hasn't experienced a great deal of darkness in their lives. It seems to come with the territory. But the truth is, you must know the darkness before you can work with light.

Although it's wonderful to believe that once you follow your purpose in life as a Lightworker all of your shadows will dissipate, it's actually a lifelong process. One positive about this though is that, as you become more experienced, you can work through any issues or obstacles much faster and easier.

When you notice any negative recurring patterns in your life, even those you thought you conquered long ago, or events from your past start taking up residence in your mind again, it's time to work on those shadows.

I mentioned earlier that I wrote a book on Shadow Work, but I'll share some steps here:

- Ask yourself what the pattern or issue is and label it. It could be something like, "Bullied in elementary school", "Alcoholic father", "Eating disorder as a young adult", or whatever shadow is coming up for you.

- Ask yourself what emotion is tied to this issue or pattern. Is it fear? Guilt? Shame? Anger? Sadness?

- Ask yourself where this first began in your life. You might have to think a while on this if you haven't traced the issue back to the start.

- Visualize the event in as much detail as possible. This isn't easy and can bring up a lot of old junk, but stay with it and breathe through it.

- Mentally send healing white light to this old memory and/or your younger self.

- Keep visualizing this scene and see it becoming brighter, warmer, dissolving the darkness. I often stay with this visualization until my healing light has brightened that painful memory to the point that it's like a bleached-out photo.

- At some point, you should notice your tension easing up and the negative feelings dissolving, even if just a little. Sometimes it feels like a weight is lifted from you, other times it feels like something shifts inside you, and once in a while, you might not notice anything at all. That's okay, just tell yourself that you'll eventually transform all of that darkness.

The more you work on healing and transmuting your shadows, the happier you'll be and the easier it will be to follow your life purpose and help others.

5. Ask Yourself Four Questions Every Day

It's so easy to go through our days almost mechanically at times. We typically do the same chores, the same work, and have the same routines. It can get to the point that we don't even know how we're feeling from one moment to the next as we become numb to any happiness and lose sight of our goals.

Living in the present is the best way to wake yourself up, boost your intuition, and strengthen your energy field. To do this, get into the habit of asking yourself the following questions each day. It doesn't matter when you do it. You can ask yourself these questions in the morning, afternoon, or evening. You could even do this more than once a day.

- What are three things I see right now? (Choose one of those and spend just a moment noticing the shape, size, and color(s). If you can, pick it up and notice how it feels in your hands, the weight of it, the texture, etc.)

- What can I hear right now? (Close your eyes and listen to the sounds around you. Mentally name each one. Pause a moment to see if there are other sounds you didn't notice at first that might be subtler.)

- How do I feel right now? (Tune in to the physical sensations in your body and your emotions. What feels good? What feels off or painful? Do any areas feel tense? Are you feeling tired, stressed, sad, worried, eager, happy, hungry, etc.?)

- What do I need right now? (Sometimes it could be as simple as needing a glass of water, a five-minute stretch, a relaxing bath, or a hug. Other times it could be something you've been putting off such as eating healthier, getting a yearly physical, having a difficult conversation with someone important to you, or saving up for a much-needed vacation.)

Noticing sights and sounds in your immediate environment helps you to tune into the here and now rather than where we typically are with our thoughts. Asking the last two questions helps you to get in touch with your current feelings and true needs.

You might be surprised to find out what it is you're feeling and desiring once you begin asking yourself directly. It also stops you from going through the motions like most people who are living their life on autopilot. This is one of my favorite ways to stay in alignment with myself.

Lightworkers are so empathetic and their hearts are wide open, which is why self-care is so important. It's far too easy to focus on the wants and needs of others or to shut ourselves off and go through our days half asleep. What a waste that is. You've come into this world to do beautiful work, but be sure you're taking care of yourself first and foremost before you take care of others.

Raising Your Energy Frequency

As a Lightworker you have a natural-born talent to manifest things. You don't have to read a single article or book about the law of attraction because, at a subconscious level, you're doing this every day without realizing it. The problem is, you probably haven't manifested the things you truly want.

Instead, because you've been working with your energy incorrectly, you've attracted what you fear most or what you've become accustomed to. We all want positive opportunities and people in our lives, but we unconsciously stick to the well-worn path we've always known, even if we have big goals and dreams for ourselves. Now that you're realizing your true role in life as a Lightworker, it's time to start making good things happen and manifesting your desired outcome.

Everything is made of energy, it's only in our three-dimensional world where that energy takes physical form. *You* are made of energy and, as a Lightworker, your energy would normally vibrate at a higher frequency than most others'. Too often though we allow the past, our stressful experiences, and negative people to drag down our energy levels. This energy is then sent out into the Universe and you'll receive in return the things that vibrate at that same frequency. Makes sense, right?

Whatever and whomever you have in your life now and in the past is what you've manifested with the frequency your energy level is vibrating at. At first, that might sound frustrating, scary, or even disheartening. If you look at it from another angle though, it shows just how powerful you truly are! Now that you know this, it's time to take responsibility and get to work at making wonderful things happen for yourself and others.

So how do you change your energy frequency and manifest like a true Lightworker? Your first step is, in everything you do, it must come from a place of love and peace. Allowing fear, greed, desperation, or envy into the equation is how you've attracted everything you don't want in your life. It's why your finances are precarious, you're in a job you can't stand, or are in a dysfunctional relationship.

Trust me, I'm not trying to blame you or pile the guilt on. I know how difficult life can be and I've been in those situations and more. But once I realized and accepted that I was the one attracting and keeping this junk in my life is when I was finally set free and able to manifest wonderful people and opportunities at long last.

Many Lightworkers I've talked to, whether they've been doing it for just a few months or for decades, believe that in order to do our true work we need to sacrifice our time, health, and happiness. Nothing could be further from the truth. You can't help others to be their best if you aren't your best.

Enlightened Lightworkers know that taking care of their own needs—finances, health, love, career, and home—will enable them to help humanity so much better. We need to lead by example and show others that success and happiness are available to all.

When you operate from a genuine place of enlightenment, have trust in the Universe, and have faith in the role you've been chosen for, you'll find that you begin manifesting the things that truly matter. I'm always surprised and often in awe as to what the Universe sends into my life. Very often it's things I never knew I needed or would have thought about asking for.

Years ago I honestly felt I needed a lot of money, six figures or more, to have the life I dreamed of. With a lot of hard work and dedication I did just that. But you know what? I wasn't any happier than I had been. Not only that, but trying to stay at that level was stressful and burned me out so badly I had to take a good chunk of time off just to build up my health again. All of that money and the work I was doing was in no way in alignment with my role as a Lightworker.

Fast forward to my life now and, although it might seem modest by some peoples' standards, I've never been happier. I have a cozy home, a beautiful yard with lots of wildlife and gardens, work that inspires and excites me, and I'm able to spend quality time with my friends and loved ones. I'm also helping others in bigger ways than I ever had before. These are the things that have always truly mattered to me.

I wouldn't trade this time in my life for anything, certainly not for that big house and big bank account I *thought* I needed years ago. Once I let go of my ego-driven wants, my energy frequency naturally rose several notches and I manifested, with very little effort, everything I truly needed for my highest good and ultimate happiness.

Ask yourself what it is that you really want in life. It's easy to say something like, "more money", but dig deeper and find out why you feel you need it. It's usually not the money itself, but what money can bring into your life, right?

On the surface, it might seem like we want one thing, but very often what we really desire is to be able to do, solve, or experience something. Using myself as an example and my previous quest for a six-figure income, I wanted it because I believed that having all that money would:

- Allow me to move into a nicer, bigger home. (In reality, it was expensive, too much room for our needs and too much upkeep.)

- Allow me to take my family on nice vacations. (We did, and the memories are great, but we would have all been just as happy doing something else that didn't cost so much.)

- Allow me to work less. (That backfired completely. I had to continually work 60+ hours a week to keep that kind of money rolling in.)

- Allow me to feel less stressed. (While I was no longer worried about how to pay my rent and bills, I was more stressed than ever.)

One plus though was that it showed me just how good I was at manifesting what I wanted in life. So, rather than focusing on money, I turned my goals around and realized that what I really wanted was financial stability, a home to feel happy in, less work so I had more time with my family, and more time for hobbies and volunteering.

Those are the things I truly wanted and have since manifested in my life and then some. And, I honestly didn't have to do much to make it happen. It was as if, as soon as everything clicked into place in my heart, mind, and soul, the opportunities unfolded right before me. Sure, I didn't always know where a path would lead, but I had trust in myself and the Universe to get me to the right place. And here I am.

So, ask yourself what you want, why you want it, how it will help you and others, then release your ego and let your higher self get to work at creating it for you. It *will* happen!

Manifesting Like A Lightworker

As a Lightworker, I want you to know just how powerful you are at manifesting and that you have the potential to create the life you need. If you don't like where you're at now, remind yourself that this is a direct reflection of the immense energy you've been putting out. Most people aren't aware that they're doing this though and by default are beaming out a mixture of vibrations that include:

- Fear

- Hope

- Desire

- Worry

- Anger

- Frustration

- Resentment

- Envy

- Desperation

- Love

Is it any wonder that so many of us continually live a life of instability? However, just the fact that you're waking up more and more to your path of being a Lightworker will help you change all of that. Soon you'll find that you have more control over your manifestations, and yet most of the time they'll take place naturally.

So, how do you release those negative, fear-based energies that are holding you back? The answer might sound far too simple, but all you need to do is allow your awakening to continue to happen. Don't force it. Don't try to dictate the timing or direction. Just, go with it.

Here are some things you can do that will help with the process:

- *Let go of whatever you're clinging too tightly to.*

If you're afraid of losing something (money, material items, status, etc.), or someone (romantic partner, friend, loved one) that's your ego talking. This type of fear is never healthy and only brings you stress and worry. In the past, I would worry about one of my daughters dying or my significant other cheating, or any number of "lower vibrational" things like this. I was constantly living life in a state of high anxiety. Once I learned to let go and realize that so many things are out of my control it felt amazing. I also found that nearly everything I worried about never happened. All it added up to was wasted time and energy.

- *Release the negative, however slowly, but surely.*

Cut cords with the old part of you that used to attract those types of people and events. This will take time so be patient with yourself. You didn't learn your patterns overnight and they won't disappear like a puff of smoke. When you catch yourself doing or saying something that isn't for your highest good stop and make a different decision that will put you back on the right path.

- Choose to surround yourself with as much positivity as possible.

This includes people, food, work, activities, and your home. Again, this isn't easy at first, but the more you release the negative and embrace the positive, no matter how small those steps are at first, it gets easier over time. I've had to let go of negative friends who were psychic vampires, keep certain foods out of the house because I can't control myself (such as donuts, cake, and pies), find a job that didn't make me miserable, and get rid of too much stuff in my home.

- Do more things that bring you happiness and peace.

In the past, I would put off doing something I loved such as taking a walk in nature, working in the yard, playing with my dog, cooking a new recipe, volunteering, or doing one of my craft projects just to squeeze in more work. How awful is that? Think of all the things you're missing out on that could be raising your energy frequency and bringing you more joy. When your time comes to leave this current life will you regret not having worked more? I seriously doubt that.

- Whatever you choose to do, be sure it resonates, feels comfortable, and is relatively easy.

You won't keep following a path, regardless of how amazing it might seem, if it isn't in alignment with who you truly are at a soul level. As I mentioned, that six-figure income did not come easy for me. It was hard work that just about destroyed me. It also kept me away from the things and people I wanted to spend more time with. Once I began following things that brought me happiness in all the ways that mattered, it was nearly effortless.

Where you are now is probably a whole lot different than where you'll be a few years from now. I'm certainly proof of that! As you continue to do more things that are in alignment with your true self your vibration will naturally change. Eventually, you'll no longer be operating on a level of negativity that was programmed into you by your parents, teachers, peers, and past events.

Yes, you've learned valuable lessons and you wouldn't be who you are, the Lightworker you're meant to be, if you didn't go through those situations, but you no longer need to carry it all around. Your energy frequency is meant to be so much higher and brighter, and it will be. Soon you'll notice that what you give out you'll receive ... and it will be amazing.

Attracting What You Need

Along with working on changing your old habits and patterns that have attracted so much of what you *don't* want into your life, there are three things I do regularly to help manifest what I truly need. Keep in mind that when you do this those gifts might not come wrapped exactly as you expect them to, but you'll receive them for a reason. Many times, what I thought I wanted was vastly different than what actually felt at home to my soul.

This probably isn't the first book you've read on attracting what you want into your life so these steps aren't anything new, but they work. The key is having faith and sticking to it. I know how disappointing it can be when you've spent so much time trying to manifest positive things into your life, but it doesn't appear. Don't give up though. If something isn't working, maybe you need to focus on another area of your life, choose something smaller at first, or tweak things a bit.

Do the following three steps every day to help attract positive people and opportunities. I usually do them right when I wake up and then again before going to bed. If I'm feeling down, stressed, or frustrated I'll do it when those feelings hit me as well. This helps me to focus on my true goals and not instant gratification or getting dragged down into a spiral of negative thinking.

1. Affirmations

It's as easy as writing down what you want in your life in the present tense, such as, "I'm in a loyal, happy, and passionate relationship" or "I'm following my path as a Lightworker and bringing in a comfortable income with it" and repeating this several times a day. The best time to do this is right when you wake up and right before going to sleep since your mind is in a partially hypnotic state at those times.

Do affirmations really work? Yes! Think of your subconscious as a great supercomputer and affirmations as new programming software designed to make changes in your life. The more you use this new "software" the faster your mind will respond to your commands. I'm sure you've heard the saying, "garbage in, garbage out", and that's how our energy to manifest things works. Unconsciously you've been sending negative or conflicting messages out into the Universe and that's why your life isn't where you want it to be.

Ask yourself what kind of outcome you truly want. What do you want to manifest in your life? Write your affirmations down in a journal, or, better yet, put them on sticky notes around your home, your car, your office, or cubicle, so you can see them throughout the day and be reminded of what you want for yourself. Here are a few affirmations to get you started, though feel free to create your own:

~ I experience joy every day of my life.

~ Every breath I take fills my body and spirit with positive energy.

~ My every need is immediately and automatically fulfilled.

~ *My mind is completely focused on my goals.*

~ *My life is filled with abundance and prosperity.*

~ *I attract love and success with ease.*

~ *I surround myself with good people and positive experiences.*

~ *Money comes easily to me and I spend it wisely.*

~ *I'm following my true calling as a Lightworker and love it.*

The list is endless as to what you can manifest, though try to keep your affirmations to only three at a time, or just one. Your mind will need time to create new neural pathways that will then feed your energy field. If you overwhelm yourself it will all backfire. You'll become frustrated and give up before you see any true benefits.

2. Visualizations

Even if you aren't sure where your negative patterns originated or how you keep attracting more of what you don't want, remind yourself that your soul is older and wiser beyond your current Earth years. Even if you do remember how you acquired money or relationship problems or whatever you're struggling with, visualization is a powerful way to heal and change everything you've repeated in life up to this point.

Close your eyes and imagine your ideal life. What would bring you the most peace and happiness? What would make you feel stable and secure? What do you really need so that you can fully embrace your life as a Lightworker and be of service to others? I want you to picture the end result, not how you got there. Trust that your higher self and the Universe will bring you what you need.

Visualize your life five or ten years from now. How do you feel? How do you look? Where do you live? What career do you have? Who are you with? Wherever you need to be healed, imagine that you have completely healed that part of yourself and you are now living life as you dreamed it could be. Try to picture this in as much detail as possible.

When I first started doing this exercise my visions were fuzzy. I couldn't really see faces or places. Instead, I felt my emotions. I felt calm yet excited, focused, and confident on my life path, filled with love and happiness. Honestly, I didn't know who would be in that future life with me. I knew my daughters would, of course, but would there be sons-in-law? A significant other? Grandchildren? Where would I be living? With whom? There were so many uncertainties and, honestly, a lot of it wasn't all that important to me. I just knew how I wanted to *feel*.

As time went on the images in my mind became stronger and, although I gave the Universe lots of wiggle room, at least I had some snapshots in my mind as to what I wanted for myself. I considered them landmarks on my life map. Mostly, I saw myself relaxed, smiling, and fulfilled on many levels doing the things I love with the people I love.

If anything was possible and nothing could get in your way, what would you see for yourself in the future? How do you want to feel? What would be your landmarks, letting you know you're on the right path or have arrived?

When you do your visualization go crazy with it. Dream big! Imagine immensely! Conjure up the images and experiences of what you want and imagine yourself already having those things or experiences. Most importantly, try to steep yourself in the emotions associated with the experiences you wish for yourself.

Once you have a loose idea or even a well-focused one, do this visualization every day, even twice or three times a day if you can. If you do it before you go to sleep at night, it will have a greater impact since your mind and higher self can "sleep on it" and your conscious mind won't be getting in the way.

Soon you may find that you're sleeping better, feel more refreshed, happier, lighter, even wiser. The issues you have or negative situations you're in will eventually lessen over time as you naturally attract and gravitate toward your life as a Lightworker.

3. Take Action

When you start putting your new energy out into the Universe stand back and allow things to flow naturally then take action when opportunities present themselves. Try not to get too hung up on how things will happen, when they will happen, or how it will look. Many times, a wondrous new path starts out very small and seems almost insignificant or might look nothing as you imagined it would.

Have faith that your higher self will guide you to the people, circumstances, and steps necessary to get you what you want and where you want to be. What I've found though is that when things are meant to happen it's serendipitous and nothing needs to be forced. It unfolds almost magically.

It's easy for our lower Earth selves to get involved though. We're presented with something and either read too much into it, try to force it, or completely disregard it as something trivial. Keep an open mind and if something sparks an interest in you or perks up your intuition, look more into it. Take action and keep pursuing it as long as it feels positive and in alignment with who you are at a soul level.

As you pursue your role as a Lightworker—in your own life and the lives of others—you'll get better and better at manifesting what you need to shine brighter.

FAQs

Before I end this book I want to cover some frequently asked questions as it relates to following the path of a Lightworker.

How will I know I'm ready?

Waiting until you feel 100% confident to pursue your path as a Lightworker is a huge mistake. For most of us, we never feel completely ready and that's because, as a human being and a soul, you're meant to learn and grow constantly. For nearly all of us we either jump into this and adjust the course over time or take on tasks little by little then increase our work as the years go by.

There will be times when you feel very confident and times when you wonder, "what am I doing here!" Just keep in mind that a lack of confidence or too much confidence is your ego coming through—either as fear or pride. Tuck aside any uncertainties and simply do good work and your life's mission(s) will be set before you.

My advice is to start somewhere, anywhere, no matter how seemingly small the path appears at first. Just doing some type of good in the world, whatever it is, will increase your energy field and therefore widen your path as a Lightworker.

What type of Lightwork should I do?

This varies from person to person and can change slightly or dramatically throughout the years. You don't have to be the president of an international charity, devote 23 hours a day, or stress over what you should be doing. Instead, wherever you see a chance to make a positive impact, do it. Even the littlest tasks add up.

I've known Lightworkers whose days were filled with responsibilities such as raising a family, or working full time, or going to school full time, and so on. But they still found opportunities each day to make an impact. This might include:

- Cooking a meal for an ill or injured friend, family member, or neighbor

- Knitting or crocheting items for shelters or charities

- Sharing vegetables from your garden with neighbors or a shelter

- Babysitting for a friend or relative who needs some me-time

- House-sitting/pet-sitting if someone you know is in the hospital

- Teaching a child or elderly neighbor a new skill

- Doing an errand for someone unable to do it themselves

The list is endless as to the small things you can do daily that add up to big Lightwork over time. If you want to do something more formal or on a bigger scale, you could pursue one of the paths we talked about earlier: teaching, counseling, writing, art, music, healthcare, etc.

What if I start on this path and don't like it?

Because Lightworkers feel so deeply it comes with the territory that we're often plagued with guilt or become easily overwhelmed. You can follow a certain path as long as you want to, whether it's days, weeks, months, years, or even decades. Then, if you no longer feel passionate about it, try something else. Your light will shine in everything you do, so never believe that you need to stick to one path and that's that.

One of my clients started out as a stay-at-home mom who would babysit others' children on occasion so the parents could get out for a bit. She then got a daycare license and did this for a few years and loved it. She then studied massage therapy and had an office she operated out of for seven years. Now she writes for a spiritual website and has written a few books. At some point, I'm sure her work will diverge yet again.

The main thing is, she pays attention to how she's feeling while on her current path and if she starts feeling stressed, burned out, or no longer passionate about it she knows it's time to find some other Lightwork to do.

A friend of mine has a regular office job but on the weekends and after hours she feeds and rescues feral cats. Sometimes she'll foster sickly cats, and she regularly volunteers at the local Humane Society.

In my own life, I've worked in the medical field, had a natural healing and counseling office, was a ghostwriter for medical and spiritual healers, was a blogger and radio show host, and now I'm an author and psychic counselor.

Again, don't worry too much about what you're meant to do. I believe that we'll all be led where we're supposed to go do to our good in the world, no matter the scale.

Isn't being a Lightworker more complicated than what you've written about?

Anything can be made far more complicated than it needs to be. I'm certain you can find a five-page discussion on how to boil an egg, but is that necessary? Or course, if you want to learn more about being a Lightworker there are many good books and websites. Sometimes it can just lead to more confusion and frustration though. I've read that there are 12+ different types of Lightworkers and there are even sub-types to those.

In reality, you're a Lightworker and that's all you need to label it as. You're here to do good in the world and help others, animals, and/or the planet in some way. Does it matter if you're a guide, a psychic, a healer, or whatever? Especially since so many of these can crossover and blend.

Also, making it more esoteric or complicated than it needs can make things more puzzling. You could think to yourself, "I'm great with animals, so I'll focus on that!" But then you discover that you're also really good at playing an instrument, or horticulture, or hands-on healing, or being calm during emergencies, or any number of talents. Why box yourself in? Being a Lightworker and following that calling wherever it might take you is all that matters.

What if my friends/family don't understand or approve of my being a Lightworker?

People tend to fear or become angry about things that are new to them or that they don't understand. Rather than having an open mind and learning something they choose to ridicule, lecture, lash out, or turn a deaf ear. Being a Lightworker can sometimes be a solitary path yet one you follow because you know it's what you need to do. Besides, how could doing positive things for the world be bad?

If your friends or family disapprove then it simply shows that they're operating at a lower energy frequency. There's nothing you can do about that, but don't let it deter you from your mission in this lifetime.

If they're somewhat open to listening, give them the shortened version and just say that you feel very passionate about (whatever you feel compelled to follow) and that this is your life to live. If they're very open to listening, then speak from your heart and let your light shine. Tell them how excited you are about your new mission in life and share some of your goals and dreams. Your happiness should mean more to them than what you choose to pursue.

I'm just me, am I really meant to be a Lightworker?

Being humble is often at the center of every Lightworker. That's why it's hard to believe that you truly are someone special and meant to do more than just go through life on autopilot. I've been a psychic counselor for well over twenty years now and I still have moments where I say to myself, "What makes me so special? Why was I chosen to have this gift and offer it to others?" I then laugh at my uncertain, fragile self that popped up and remember how blessed and passionate I feel about the path I'm on.

You don't need a Ph.D. or to be voted into office to be a Lightworker. You can be you, doing your work, in any way that makes you happy and helps others in some way. Nobody in this world has lived your life and can offer assistance in exactly the way you can. Every Lightworker is unique, regardless of what path they're following and how many others are doing the seemingly exact same thing.

Is it greedy or against my higher calling in life to be paid as a Lightworker?

You need money to survive in this world, plain and simple. Some Lightworkers choose to keep their regular job and volunteer in their off-time. Some make a living doing some type of Lightwork (teaching, counseling, divination, etc.) and choose to volunteer or do other good work in their spare time. While many have regular 9 – 5 jobs and make money as a part-time Lightworker.

It's not wrong to be paid for your services. You shouldn't feel guilty charging a living wage if you have something of value to offer others. The only time negativity could creep into this is if you aren't operating from a higher place and for the good of all involved.

I've known of psychics predicting awful tragedies for people or telling them they've had a curse placed on them, only to charge them huge fees to clear their client, protect them, or "change the future". I've also known doctors, who are supposed to focus on healing and helping, give false diagnoses so the patient keeps coming back. I've known people in many other helping or healing careers who unnecessarily instill fear or give false information just to charge far more money than they should be.

Yes, you need to know your worth and charge accordingly, but at the center of it all is our deep desire to be of service and to make things better. So, don't feel guilty about making money as a Lightworker, but stay positive, humble yet confident, and honest.

What should I do if my path starts becoming overwhelming or stressful?

This can happen for a few reasons:

- You might have chosen a path that doesn't really resonate with you at a soul level.

For me, I always thought I wanted to work in the medical field. I went to school for it, excelled in my studies, then discovered that I didn't care for it at all when I actually started doing the work.

At my very core, I've always wanted to help others heal so it was natural for me to believe I should enter into the healthcare arena. Over time I realized that what I really wanted to do was to help others through the confusion and emotional upheavals of life, and to light their way through the darkness.

- You might have started your path too quickly or jumped into the deep end without gaining enough experience or knowledge first.

Regardless of where you end up during your journey as a Lightworker, you always need to start at the beginning. A client of mine learned that lesson the hard way. She wanted to help others and had a deep love for natural healing and spirituality. Without making a plan or even knowing exactly what she wanted to do she got a one-year lease for a storefront, bought everything from crystals and herbs to tarot cards and capes, and advertised that she did readings as well.

Though her heart was in the right place and her eagerness was admirable, she had only done readings for herself in the past and had no idea how to run a business. Needless to say, it went badly and she went into debt. Her shop closed down six months later and she got some bad reviews online. Her confidence was badly shaken for a while, but she recovered and now does angel readings at a local New Age store and loves it.

While it's true that many things a Lightworker can do require almost no training or money, some of them do. Just be sure you prepare yourself before taking those first steps. It's better to work your way up rather than sliding your way down.

- You're doing too much

As a Lightworker it's easy to give, give, and give some more. We love helping so much that it can become an obsession or obligation. Neither of those is helpful. It's best to pace yourself, figure out how much time and energy you can comfortably devote to your mission, and always check in with yourself to see how you're feeling.

When I first started doing readings there were days I would do 10 or more. I'd be drained down to my soul afterward and started feeling resentful about this gift that felt more like a curse. Of course, that was just my ego throwing a fit. I admitted to myself that doing so many readings a day wasn't helpful to my clients or myself. How could I offer my best if I felt at my worst and was always in a mad rush?

What I ended up doing was raising my prices and letting clients know that it could be a few days before I got back to them. And you know what? It didn't hurt my business in the least. It's also helped me to be a better psychic counselor and I don't feel drained or stressed anymore. It's also given me more time to work on my writing, which is another passion of mine.

While you do your work, regardless of what it is, never overwhelm yourself. It's better to help one person to the best of your ability than a thousand people while you're feeling burned out.

- You aren't focusing on self-care first and foremost.

Self-care includes taking time out to decompress, relax, heal, have fun, and strengthen yourself. When you put everyone else first where does that leave you? You're either at the bottom of the list or not even on it. This can lead to stress, resentment, and ultimately giving up on your path as a Lightworker because you're worn out and worn down.

It's not selfish to focus on your mental, physical, emotional, and spiritual health. Not only is it a necessity but it will make you an even better Lightworker. When you show respect for yourself others will respect and appreciate you far more.

What if I have a question that isn't covered in this book?

Although I tried to include as much information as I could in this short book, I understand that you might have something on your mind that isn't in here. If so, feel free to contact me any time at: Dr.Kelly.Psychic.Counselor@gmail.com I'd also love to hear about the Lightwork you're currently doing or plan to do soon.

I hope you've found *Way Of The Lightworker - Discovering Your Role & Following Your Path As A Healing Guide* enlightening and exciting. The world needs more of us so refuse to hold yourself back! I can guarantee that it will be one of the most rewarding things you'll ever do in this lifetime—and future ones as well.

Contact Me/Book A Reading

Whether your problems or concerns are in the areas of love, finances, family, career, health, education, or your path in life, I offer professional intuitive counseling, caring guidance, and solutions that work!

I use no tools. Instead, I'll connect directly with your higher self and your spirit guides to help you through any situation and achieve the best possible results. No problem is too big or too small, and your questions will be answered in detail.

I'll let you know absolutely everything that comes through in the reading which typically includes past, present, and future energies, guidance, time frames and predictions. Each reading is in-depth, filled with positive energy and guidance, and includes one free clarification email.

All readings are done via email. By offering my readings through email you'll be able to save your reading and go back to it again and again for guidance.

I look forward to reading for you!

Check out my readings, books, blog posts, and more on my website:

D[1]rKellyPsychic.com

Or email me directly at: DrKellyPsychicCounselor@gmail.com

---

1. http://psychicreadingsbydrkelly.webs.com/psychic-readings